Empathetic Entrepreneurs

Raising Kids to Change the World

Table of Contents

Chapter 1. Introduction

Welcome to an enlightening exploration that is sure to impact the way you raise your children—our Special Report on "Empathetic Entrepreneurs: Raising Kids to Change the World". This captivating piece delves into the magical realm of teaching empathy and entrepreneurial spirit to the younger generation, preparing them not just to succeed, but to make a meaningful difference. Rather than serving up dry theory, we share heartwarming stories of children who, equipped with compassion and business acumen, are already shaping our world. Our interviews with their parents and mentors provide invaluable guidance for your own journey. This report is more than informative – it's positively inspirational! Don't miss the chance to empower your kids with the tools and the mindset they need to create the world of their dreams!

Chapter 2. The Power of Empathy in Leadership

Empathy has long been seen as a soft skill, however, in the entrepreneurial world, it's now recognized as a vital source of leadership strength. The ability to understand and share the feelings of another person helps in fostering genuine connections – a trait that infuses warmth into business relationships and yields significant results.

2.1. Creating a Culture of Empathy

Building an empathetic environment within your organization begins at the top. If leaders can empathize with their staff, they can create a positive workplace atmosphere, reinforcing the significance of each team member's role and its relationship to the company's mission. The process instills a sense of pride and purpose among employees, leading to enhanced productivity.

Consider the example of a young entrepreneur named Maya. When she launched her start-up, she had one overarching goal: to create a company culture that was as empathetic as it was ambitious. She took time to learn about her team members' individual strengths, weaknesses, aspirations, and fears, and acted accordingly. The results were formidable. The employees, feeling valued, put their hearts and souls into their work. The company didn't just survive its difficult start-up phase – it thrived.

2.2. Empathy and Customer Relations

Emphasizing empathy doesn't just help create an inclusive team environment; it also affects how the company interacts with its customers. When your business can understand the customer's perspective, it can offer solutions that more accurately meet their needs, which in turn leads to higher customer satisfaction.

We see this principle in action with Rahul, a teenage entrepreneur with a knack for empathizing with his customers. His technology startup designs user-friendly apps, and Rahul has always made it a point to try and put himself in the shoes of the end-user. The result? His apps offer a seamless user experience that resonates with their target audience, earning him rave reviews and helping his company scale quickly.

2.3. Reaping the Benefits of Compassionate Leadership

Empathy breeds passion and dedication, two vital qualities for any startup hoping to make its mark. Leaders who show compassion will inspire their teams to push boundaries, embracing creativity and innovation.

Take Sophia as an example. With a dream of launching a social enterprise, she has always taken an empathetic leadership style, keen to demonstrate an understanding of her team's needs and inspirations. Sophia's team members, feeling respected and understood, became more invested in the company's success. Harnessing this dedication, Sophia's organization took off, tackling pressing societal problems and making a real impact.

2.4. Nurturing Young Empathetic Leaders

To nurture empathy in young leaders, it's crucial to create an environment that values emotional literacy. Encouraging open dialogue about feelings can help them understand and regulate their emotions better, leading them to become more empathetic over time.

Zain, at thirteen, is on the path to becoming an empathetic entrepreneur. His parents have always encouraged open discussions about emotions in their household, teaching Zain to express himself and understand others. Now heading a successful non-profit for environmental conservation, Zain's empathetic approach has won him the support and admiration of many.

In the end, we find that empathy, when coupled with a sound business strategy, can pave the way for robust, sustainable growth in an enterprise. Leaders who can empathize can inspire, and such inspiration can lead to great things. As we raise the future generation of entrepreneurs, let's be sure to put empathy up there with the other business skills in our toolkit. In the ever-challenging world of startups, the absolute power empathy commands may just be the special ingredient that tips the balance towards success.

Chapter 3. Entrepreneurship: More than Money Making

An entrepreneurial journey is often seen to be all about making money, but in truth, it is much more than that. While it does play a pivotal role, the undeniable fact remains that entrepreneurship is about making a difference, about changing the status quo, and, more importantly, about providing solutions to the problems that society faces. It is a journey of growth, innovation, opportunity, and one that does not necessarily have to start as an adult. It can start in childhood.

3.1. The Value of Entrepreneurship Beyond Monetary Gain

Many adults view entrepreneurship purely from a financial perspective, which is understandable given that money is a way to quantify success. But the impact of entrepreneurship extends far beyond the individual entrepreneur. Entrepreneurship drives economic growth, fosters innovation, and creates employment opportunities. However, what makes entrepreneurship truly unique is that it instills a forward-thinking, problem-solving mindset. It teaches resilience, adaptability, and independence — qualities that are not only vital in business but also in life.

A quick glance at history reveals numerous successful entrepreneurs who have impacted society significantly through their disruptive innovations. From Steve Jobs to Elon Musk, their visionary approaches towards business have shaped the way the world works.

As you teach your kids about entrepreneurship, remember that financial success is merely the tip of the iceberg. The real value of entrepreneurship consists of the skills they acquire, the mindset they develop, and the positive impact they can have on society.

3.2. Cultivating a Problem-Solving Mindset

The difference between a business and a successful entrepreneurial venture is problem-solving. Entrepreneurs don't simply provide goods or services; they offer solutions. Children yanked out of their comfort zones and thrust into the intriguing world of entrepreneurship quickly learn to look at the world differently. Instead of complaining about problems, they begin to see them as opportunities for innovation. This, in turn, cultivates critical thinking, creativity, and resourcefulness.

In teaching your kids about entrepreneurship, allow them to identify a problem they're passionate about solving. Ignite their natural curiosity by encouraging them to explore solutions. Remember to expose them to the necessary process of trial and error. Mistakes are not failures, but rather essential stepping stones on the path to success.

3.3. The Spirit of Resilience and Perseverance

Resilience and perseverance are two critical traits that all successful entrepreneurs possess. Learning how to manage failure and keep going despite challenging circumstances is a wonderful lesson for kids. They learn to view setbacks as an opportunity to revisit their approach and make necessary adjustments.

The story of Thomas Edison and his journey to invent the electric light bulb is a perfect example of resilience and perseverance. After thousands of unsuccessful attempts, when asked about his failure, Edison said, "I have not failed. I've just found 10,000 ways that won't work." Teaching children stories like these will inspire them to accept failure as part of the process and not a reflection of their abilities.

3.4. Empathy: The Heart of an Entrepreneaur

Entrepreneurship isn't all about technical skills and business strategies. It is also about connecting with people on a root level. Empathy – the ability to understand and share the feelings of others – is an essential competency in entrepreneurship. Empathetic entrepreneurs can resonate with their customers' needs and respond effectively. By teaching kids to be empathetic, we're grooming them to be customer-centric entrepreneurs.

There are several ways to nurture empathy in children. We can model empathy by practicing it in our daily interactions. Also, encourage them to consider diverse perspectives, engage in community service, and read books that explore emotions.

Ignite the entrepreneurial spirit in your kids, allow them the room to grow, make mistakes, learn, and eventually see the bigger picture. With the right mindset and skills, they can leverage their business acumen to create positive change in society, proving that entrepreneurship is indeed more than just about money-making. Remember, the children of today are the leaders of tomorrow, and it's upon us to shape them into individuals who can make a difference globally.

Chapter 4. The Intersection of Compassion and Commerce

In our modern world, there are two key attributes that often distinguish successful individuals — their ability to empathize and innovate. These factors harness transformative power, especially when they intersect in entrepreneurial ventures. When compassion serves as the bedrock of commerce, it has the potential to lead to profound societal changes.

4.1. The Compassionate Perspective

Empathetic entrepreneurs often start by seeing the world through a compassionate lens. They recognize the profound interconnectedness of all individuals and understand that our commonality is our shared humanity. This perspective becomes their driving force in designing solutions that not only address people's needs but also affirm their dignity and worth.

One such child was Sarah, a ten-year-old from Ohio. She noticed several people in her community could not afford basic food necessities. Instead of dismissing the situation as unchangeable, Sarah sought to understand, translating her empathy into action. With a small allowance and support from her family, she initiated a neighborhood-wide food drive. What started as a basic act of empathy soon led to the establishment of 'Share-A-Bite', a mini social entreprise, distributing surplus produce from local farms to needy families.

Her father shared in an interview, "I've never seen such passion and dedication in someone her age. She organizes everything herself - from sourcing food to distribution. More importantly, she has never lost sight of why she does it - to ensure everyone in our community has access to food."

4.2. Empathetic Entrepreneurship – A Force for Good

Those nurturing children like Sarah are creating a new breed of entrepreneurs that redefine success. For such empathetic entrepreneurs, profit is not the sole endgame. It's about creating value that leads to lasting societal change.

Let's consider Jack, a 16-year-old from Seattle, passionate about technology. When he understood the struggles of the hearing-impaired, including his own cousin, he became determined to make a difference. Using his coding skills, Jack designed an app to convert spoken language into sign language in real-time. With a team of his peers and seed funding from a local competition, Jack's innovative enterprise is now impacting hundreds of lives.

His mother explained, "I think what sets Jack apart is his focus on serving a community. He's always talking about how his business can help more people, not just make more money."

4.3. Cultivating Empathy: The First Step

So, how are these children so different? The key lies with their caregivers who instilled empathy at a young age. By teaching their children to think about how others feel, they've empowered them to approach problem-solving with a compassionate perspective.

One excellent example is a family exercise where parents and children share their daily highs and lows. This simple yet profound tradition can encourage children to identify and respect divergent emotions and perspectives. Over time, lessons like these can motivate them to change the world one small action at a time.

4.4. Fostering Entrepreneurial Spirit: The Second Step

Instilling empathy is essential, but it's only half of the equation. The other half involves fostering an entrepreneurial spirit—imagination turned into innovation. Through experience-based learning, problem-solving exercises, and a healthy dose of guidance, parents can nurture this vital skill.

Take a look at 'KidPreneurs' – a weekend program where children engage in mock businesses, learning about capital, revenue, and profit while managing their own mini-enterprises. Besides the business aspect, the curriculum incorporates lessons on corporate social responsibility and sustainable practices. These programs illustrate that making money and making a difference are not mutually exclusive.

4.5. Transforming Vision into Reality

For a child to truly embody the spirit of an empathetic entrepreneur, they must learn how to convert their compassionate insights and innovative ideas into something tangible, something real.

In Sarah's case, her parents supported her vision by driving her to pick up first food donations, stressing the notion of 'social entrepreneurship.' With Jack, his parents encouraged skills development, enrolling him in a programming course when he showed an interest in coding.

4.6. The Future of Entrepreneurship: Shaping a Compassionate Economy

Our world has never been more ready for empathetic entrepreneurs. By fostering these values from a young age, parents can help shape their children into instrumental forces of positive change. The journey towards cultivating empathetic entrepreneurs is challenging yet rewarding, with the potential to birth a more compassionate and equitable economy.

In the end, raising children to become compassionate entrepreneurs is about inspiring them to navigate the world with both their hearts and minds open. They learn that change begins with understanding, and true success is not measured just by the value they gain, but by the value they give back to the world.

Chapter 5. Teaching Kids to Understand and Share Feelings

Understanding and sharing feelings can be a challenging concept for children to grasp. Parents and caregivers often wonder when and how to start the discussion. The key lies in making it an ongoing conversation rather than a one-time lesson. Hence, demonstrating empathy should become a daily routine, like brushing teeth or reading bedtime stories.

5.1. Empathy: An Introduction

Empathy is the ability to understand and share the feelings of others. It's a fundamental human attribute that enables us to perceive the emotions, perspectives, and experiences of people around us. Empathy bridges the gap between self and others, builds connections, and fosters compassionate actions.

Being empathetic doesn't merely mean being able to recognize particular feelings in others but also involves responding to these emotions adequately. Empathetic responses can range from words of comfort and acts of kindness to simply silent companionship during tough times.

5.2. The Development of Empathy in Children

Children's capacity for empathy develops over time, and reflects their broader emotional and cognitive development.

For instance, toddlers begin to show signs of empathy by offering a toy or hug to others who appear upset. As they grow older, they start to better understand their own emotions, which paves the way for understanding others' feelings. By school age, children can typically comprehend that different people can have different feelings about the same situation.

Parents can foster empathy through their daily interactions with their children, intentionally creating situations for empathetic discussions and actions.

5.3. Building an Emotional Vocabulary

One crucial aspect of fostering empathy in children is helping them build an emotional vocabulary. They need to be able to put their own feelings into words before they can understand how someone else might be feeling.

From a young age, talk about feelings with your child using as broad a range of emotional vocabulary as possible. Use real-life circumstances to name emotions - 'You seemed upset when your friend took your toy', or 'You seemed so proud when you finished that puzzle'. Picture books can also help in this task by visually representing different feelings.

5.4. Emotional Intelligence: Beyond Vocabulary

Building an emotional vocabulary is an indispensable part of the journey but it's emotional intelligence that allows children to navigate their feelings competently. Emotional intelligence pertains not only to understanding and expressing one's emotions but managing them effectively.

Resilience, for instance, is an aspect of emotional intelligence. Helping your child understand that everyone faces challenges, and recovering from them is part of life, can foster resilience—a crucial skill for entrepreneurs.

Teach your child about patience and perseverance, especially in moments of discomfort. Involve them in problem-solving activities to develop their ability to rationally deal with adversities.

5.5. Inspiring Action through Empathy

Understanding and sharing feelings are vital, but empathy reaches its full potential when it inspires action. These actions can be as simple as using kind words, helping an upset friend, or as complex as a business idea to solve a pervasive issue.

Role modeling is paramount in this context. Displaying empathy towards others and towards your child can inspire them to act empathetically. Recognize and commend your child's empathetic actions to reinforce their importance.

Empathy-led actions foster social consciousness—an important trait for entrepreneurs wishing to drive societal change.

5.6. Empathy and Entrepreneurship: The Connection

Empathy is an imperative trait for successful entrepreneurs as they have to understand their customers or beneficiaries to serve them effectively. Furthermore, empathy enables long-term, positive impact, driving entrepreneurs to solve real, lived problems rather than just creating profitable products or services.

Moreover, empathy also encourages collaboration—another key aspect of entrepreneurship. By understanding and valuing the emotions and perspectives of team members, one can foster an inclusive and productive team environment.

5.7. Playing the Long Game

Remember, nurturing empathy is a long-term commitment. It's not a milestone that your child reaches at a specific age but an ongoing development process. This journey can be difficult at times, and there can be setbacks, but patience and consistency can yield surprising results.

Give your child the time they need to understand, practice, and internalize empathy. And remember that you are right there with them, strengthening your empathetic ability as you help them strengthen theirs.

By raising children who understand, share, and act on feelings, we are planting the seeds for a generation of empathetic entrepreneurs who will change the world—one kind act and one sustainable business at a time.

Chapter 6. Case Studies: Young Empathetic Entrepreneurs in Action

In the wake of the technological revolution and the myriad societal challenges that come with it, a new wave of young entrepreneurs is emerging. These individuals are not just ambitious and innovative, but empathetic, conscientious, and socially aware. They strive to solve real-world problems and make a significant impact on their communities and beyond. In this chapter, we will delve into the fascinating journeys of five young empathetic entrepreneurs and how their parents and mentors have guided them.

6.1. Empathetic Young Entrepreneur: Sofia

Our first case study centers around Sofia, a 12-year-old who transformed her love for animals into a lucrative business. Sofia was deeply affected by the number of stray dogs and cats in her neighborhood. She decided to do something about it and, with a loan from her parents, started making homemade pet treats and toys.

Sofia's parents guided her in setting up the business, from finding vendors of organic ingredients to managing her finances. More importantly, they also nurtured her commitment to donate a certain percentage of her profits to local animal shelters.

What impresses the most about Sofia's entrepreneurial journey is not only her tangible success - her products are now available in local pet stores across three neighboring towns - but also her unflinching dedication to her cause. Sofia exemplifies how entrepreneurial spirit and empathy can combine to create a sustainable, socially-conscious enterprise at a young age.

6.2. Empathetic Young Entrepreneur: Karan

Karan, a 16-year-old tech prodigy from New Delhi, India, turned his coding skills into an entrepreneurial adventure while addressing a critical issue in his city. Disturbed by the rising pollution levels, Karan designed an app that allows users to measure and track air quality in real-time in their local area.

Karan's sense of empathy was cultivated through his schooling and upbringing. His family encouraged him to look beyond personal benefit and consider the broader social implications of his abilities. The guidance from his mentors and support from his parents turned his app into a profitable venture that sold air purifiers.

Karan's venture is a perfect combination of personal skill, entrepreneurship, and deep-rooted empathy for the environment and community welfare. His actions embody the empathetic entrepreneurial spirit, demonstrating that business success and societal impact can indeed go hand in hand.

6.3. Empathetic Young Entrepreneur: Amara

In the United States, 13-year-old Amara saw the difficulties her neighborhood faced when the local grocery store closed down. Many of her neighbors had no personal vehicles, and the next closest store was miles away.

Recognizing this problem, Amara devised a plan to start a mobile grocery store. She filled a refurbished bus with fresh produce and everyday essentials, creating a "grocery store on wheels." Her parents, who own a farm, supported her by supplying fresh produce.

Amara's venture has been transformative for her neighborhood, supplying necessary goods to those who were otherwise cut off. Her understanding of their struggles, her desire to help, and her entrepreneurial spirit have made a real difference, illustrating how empathy can fuel innovative solutions to local problems.

6.4. Empathetic Young Entrepreneur: Mateo

Our next story takes us to rural Argentina, where 15-year-old Mateo turned an ecological crisis into a thriving business. Dealing with devastating soil erosion in his region due to deforestation, Mateo started producing and selling seed balls - a mix of clay, compost, and native plant seeds.

Mateo's parents, both activists in their local community, educated him about the ecological balance and its importance. This knowledge propelled him to establish a business model that directly addresses the problem at hand while also being economically viable.

Mateo's seedball initiative not only helps in restoring the local biodiversity but also employs several people from his village. His entrepreneurial journey underscores how empathy towards the environment and understanding of a local issue can spur innovative business models.

6.5. Empathetic Young Entrepreneur: Lina

Our final case study highlights Lina, a 17-year-old from Lebanon. She noticed that many girls in her community lacked access to education because of poverty and societal norms. Her observation sparked an idea to start an online tutoring platform that employs educated women in her community as tutors.

Her parents supported her idea and helped her build a network of tutors. This allowed Lina to cultivate a solid customer base and establish a robust online platform.

Lina's initiative is shining a light on the importance of education for girls and women in her community while also providing them with economic opportunities.

Each of these empathetic entrepreneurs showcases how blending business acumen with empathy can lead to innovative solutions that positively impact society. They inspire us by showing that age is merely a number when it comes to entrepreneurship and making a difference — the key lies in the strength of one's empathy and the courage to act on it. These young entrepreneurs underline the importance of cultivating both empathy and entrepreneurship in our children to create a more understanding, compassionate, and innovative future.

Chapter 7. Parents as Pioneers: Shaping Future Leaders

In every child lies enormous potential. As parents, we bear the responsibility and privilege of guiding that potential: shaping it, nurturing it, stimulating it till it blossoms into a form capable of causing positive change. This chapter offers insights and lessons on raising your young ones to become empathetic entrepreneurs.

7.1. Choosing the Mindset

How we behave, react, sympathize, and engage with the world around us largely depends on our mindset. It's this mindset that parents need to identify, cultivate, and solidify in their children from an early age. Encouraging an entrepreneurial mindset means promoting resourcefulness, resilience, creativity, and optimism. Similarly, fostering empathy signifies sowing seeds of kindness, compassion, and understanding.

Balancing these two seemingly different traits might appear challenging, but they beautifully complement each other. An empathetic entrepreneur doesn't only strive for individual success but aims to uplift others along the way. By sympathizing with people's problems and possessing the resourcefulness to offer solutions, children can contribute to societal progression in their own small or significant ways.

7.2. Creating a Supportive Environment

Not all skills come naturally. Most have to be learnt, practiced, and honed. As parents, you must cultivate an environment that lets your child become observant, ask questions, and analyze situations. Allow their curiosity to flow without restrictions; it's these tiny questions that often spark significant thought processes.

By weaving discussions and debates about social, environmental, and community-related issues into daily conversations, parents can make empathy and entrepreneurship part of everyday life. Teach them that each problem is an opportunity waiting for a solution.

7.3. Learning Through Action

Children learn best when they learn by doing, stepping out of the hypothetical realm and into practical reality. Experiential learning not only helps children understand concepts better but also grow personally and professionally. Encourage your kids to set up their mini lemonade stands, organize small community events or even create crafts to sell or donate. As they take on roles of tiny entrepreneurs, they'll develop leadership, financial literacy, decision-making, and social skills.

At the same time, instill the values of empathy by including them in philanthropic activities. Regularly participating in community service or helping those less fortunate can develop their understanding of different social realities, teaching them to inherently value compassion and kindness.

7.4. Embracing Failures

Entrepreneurial journeys are not free of obstacles. Therefore, a crucial part of raising empathetic entrepreneurs involves urging them to accept failures and learn from them. As Thomas Edison once stated, "I have not failed. I've just found 10,000 ways that won't work." It is essential kids learn this lesson early on. Guide them to view failures as steps towards success rather than dead ends, and they're more likely to keep trying, innovating, and improving.

7.5. Building Networks

Entrepreneurship thrives on networks. Encourage your children to make connections and strengthen existing ones. The art of networking isn't limited to the business world; it is a crucial life skill. It encompasses forming relationships, understanding others' perspectives, and working collaboratively toward common goals. Similarly, empathy is all about connection, giving your child their first lessons in networking.

In essence, raising empathetic entrepreneurs involves fostering a particular mindset, creating a supportive environment, learning through action, embracing failures, and building networks. As parents, these efforts are investments in your children's futures, shaping them into not just future leaders, but leaders who lead with empathy, kindness, and a determination to affect positive change. Every entrepreneurial journey they undertake, every empathetic act they perform, is a step towards a just, inclusive, and innovative world we all envisage.

Chapter 8. Integrating Empathy and Business Acumen in Education

Although empathy and business acumen may seem worlds apart, they are two essential components equally crucial to the holistic education of young change-makers. By intertwining the principles of empathy and entrepreneurship, we can endow youngsters with the ability to transform society in ways that are both beneficial and heartfelt.

8.1. Understanding Empathy and Business Acumen

Empathy refers to the ability to understand and share the feelings of others. An empathetic individual is not merely compassionate but can also put themselves in another's shoes, feeling what they feel. On the other hand, business acumen is the intrepid knack to make sharp, quick decisions that lead to successful business outcomes. It employs skills such as financial literacy, analytical reasoning, and strategic insight. However, one might wonder: isn't making profits and understanding feelings diametrically opposed? Not quite. Empathy, when merged with business acumen, can promote conscientious entrepreneurship in children, seeding businesses that serve people over profits and reinforcing the fabric of community and fellowship.

8.2. Empathy: The Emotional Quotient

In education, "emotional quotient" or EQ is gradually gaining recognition parallel to IQ. Schools worldwide are acknowledging the relevance of emotional intelligence and are incorporating it into curriculum - and for a genuine reason. High EQ aids students in managing stress, developing leadership skills, and maintaining healthier relationships. Furthermore, it underlines the value of empathetic understanding, fostering an environment where emotional well-being is as significant as academic achievement.

To cultivate empathy in children, incorporate these strategies: * Encourage an Open Emotional Dialogue: Empowering kids to express their feelings courteously and honestly can pave the way for empathetic conversations. Regularly establishing emotional check-ins can allow them to acknowledge and manage their feelings better. * Foster a Culturally Sensitive Environment: Exposing children to diverse cultures, traditions, and perspectives can cultivate a broader understanding of empathy. Encourage them to learn about various communities and their challenges to realize empathy transcends the barriers of race and culture. * Engage in Community Service: Community service can be a great tool for kids to practice empathy. Volunteering gives them a firsthand experience of others' struggles, helping them become more empathetic.

8.3. Business Acumen: The Tact of Trade

Although the thought of teaching business acumen to children may seem daunting, it's far from impractical. Entrepreneurship isn't about making concocted corporate strategies - it's about identifying a problem and solving it artistically and profitably. Endeavor to develop an entrepreneurial mindset in children, starting with these tips: * Teach Financial Literacy: This is fundamental to fostering business acumen. Explain the concepts of saving, investing, and spending through practical exercises like budgeting a weekly meal or planning a family vacation. * Encourage Problem-Solving: An excellent entrepreneur is an efficient problem-solver. Encourage analytical thinking by presenting children with different scenarios and asking them to provide solutions. * Cultivate a Business Vocabulary: Incorporate business terms in your conversations with kids. Gradually, they'll start understanding the world of business, making the realms of entrepreneurship less intimidating.

8.4. Integrating Empathy with Business Acumen

Once children grasp the foundations of empathy and business acumen, the next step is to incorporate these values together. The blend of these elements can inspire children to become "empathetic entrepreneurs," favoring business with heart and value. Here are some thoughtful ways to combine empathy with entrepreneurship in education: * Crafting Social Enterprises: Encourage children to initiate socially-conscious business models that solve a problem and benefit society. These enterprises can be small-scale, like selling handmade products to raise funds for a community center. * Role-Playing Scenarios: Engage children in role-playing exercises where they have to make business decisions considering empathy. For example, they might pretend to be restaurant owners devising policies for their staff during a pandemic. * Recognition of Ethical Businesses: Teach children to recognize and support businesses that prioritize ethics over profits. This can be done through projects where they need to analyze different companies for their social responsibility.

In conclusion, the integration of empathy and business acumen in childhood education is an inspiring step towards a future of empathetic entrepreneurs. By nurturing these qualities, we empower our children to not just forge successful careers, but become architects of a compassionate society and a sustainable future. Let us foster this amalgamation of heart and commerce to inspire a new wave of change-makers who lead with both feeling and foresight.

Chapter 9. Building a Compassionate Business: Step-by-Step Guide for Children

Understanding emotions is a critical aspect of empathy, and children are naturally good at picking up emotional states. Encourage them to identify their feelings and express them clearly. By helping them navigate their own emotions, they'll be better prepared to understand the feelings of others. This serves as a foundation for a compassionate business mindset.

A good practice to follow is to have family discussions about emotions and empathy. A dinner discussion about how everyone's day went, what made them happy or sad, how they navigated the feelings - all of this can help children recognize the importance of emotional awareness in their lives.

9.1. Encouraging Compassion in Action

Next, introduce practical ways for kids to exercise compassion. This can involve simple acts at home, like sharing toys or helping with chores, or larger community-oriented actions, such as volunteering at charitable institutions or donating to a local food bank.

Reflecting on these actions with your child is crucial. Conversations should focus on how their actions made a difference and impacted others positively. The aim is to help kids understand the tangible changes they can bring about through acts of compassion.

9.2. Modeling the Desired Behavior

It's important to remember that children learn more from what they observe than what they hear. Demonstrating empathy yourself provides a powerful lesson for them. Show kindness, maintain an open mind, and speak and act compassionately; your child will learn from these actions and mimic them.

9.3. Building on Entrepreneurial Basics

Once the child has a good understanding of empathy, the foundation of a compassionate business, the next step is to introduce them to entrepreneurship. Teach them about money - how it is earned and used, the importance of saving and investing, and how a business works.

9.4. Planting the Seeds of Ideas

Encourage your child to think of a business idea, a problem they want to solve or a product they believe people would benefit from. This can be anything - from running a lemonade stand, to creating an art piece, or inventing a game. The important thing is for the child to be passionate about it.

9.5. Building an Empathy Map

Creating an empathy map for their idea will help your child understand their potential customers better. This involves identifying who their customers are, what they need, how they feel, and how their product can help. Assist them in this task, ask guiding questions, and help them fill out each section.

9.6. Testing the Idea

Encourage your child to test their idea, share it with friends, neighbors, relatives, etc., and gather feedback. This will help them to understand that feedback, even criticism, is valuable in refining their idea.

9.7. Implementing the Idea

With a refined idea, help your child set clear goals on how to implement it. This involves planning tasks, setting timelines, determining costs, and deciding on a pricing strategy. Break down big tasks into smaller, more manageable ones, and provide guidance on how to go about them.

9.8. Financial Literacy for Budding Entrepreneurs

Financial education is a crucial part of this journey. Begin with simple concepts like earning money, saving, and budgeting, then progress onto concepts like profit, loss, investment, and return on investment. Use games, activities, or kid-friendly apps to make learning fun and engaging.

9.9. Evaluating Success

Lastly, introduce the concept of success and failure. Share with them that both are part of the journey. Teach them to measure success not only in terms of profit but also by the impact they have on people and their well-being. Encourage them also to learn from failures and draw lessons to improve.

In conclusion, raising kids to build compassionate businesses is a journey that requires a firm foundation in understanding emotions and encouraging empathy. The entrepreneurial aspect involves fostering a problem-solving mindset, creativity, financial literacy, perseverance, and resilience. The future belongs to compassionate entrepreneurs, and with the right guidance, your child can be one of them.

Chapter 10. The Role of Schools and Communities in Cultivating Empathetic Entrepreneurs

Before we dive into the deep currents of schools and communities' roles in cultivating empathetic entrepreneurs, it's essential we define a fundamental concept central to our discussion: empathetic entrepreneurship. An empathetic entrepreneur is a visionary individual who recognizes the importance of empathy in business. They're fueled by a deep understanding of their customers' needs, a desire to contribute positively to society, and a drive to pioneer innovative solutions to real-world problems.

In this context, schools and communities represent the fertile soil where the initial seeds of empathetic entrepreneurship are sowed and nurtured. They play a crucial role in shaping individuals who will leverage their understanding of the world around them to cultivate innovative enterprises that make a profound and positive impact.

10.1. Cultivating Empathy in the School Environment

It's well established, the formative years spent in school can dramatically shape a person's worldview, character, and ethos. Schools have a fundamental influence on children's emotional, social, and cognitive development. They serve as essential catalysts in nurturing traits such as empathy, compassion, problem-solving, and leadership.

Many progressive schools around the world have recognized the importance of teaching empathy as part of their curriculum, attempting to foster empathy through several means:

1. Role-playing and simulation exercises, enabling students to step into others' shoes.

2. Literature and storytelling, exposing students to diverse perspectives, helping them understand and share the feelings of others.

3. Collaborative projects where students work together, encouraging them to understand and accommodate different viewpoints.

4. Community service activities, instilling the value of contributing to society.

By providing an encouraging environment for empathetic development, schools can serve as excellent incubators for future empathetic entrepreneurs. They create a foundation that can be further built upon with entrepreneurial teaching, leading to a welter of positive outcomes for the individual, community, and broader society.

10.2. Encouraging Entrepreneurship in the Classroom

Entrepreneurship education seeks to prepare people, particularly youth, to be responsible, enterprising individuals who contribute to economic development and sustainable communities. Entrepreneurship today isn't limited to just creating startups or small businesses; it's about instilling a certain mindset – a specific way of thinking propelled by innovation and opportunity recognition.

The benefits of teaching entrepreneurship in schools extend beyond equipping students with business acumen. It fosters creativity, increases students' sense of self-efficacy, improves their leadership capabilities, and prepares them to be problem solvers who can make significant contributions to their communities and larger society.

Entrepreneurship-education initiatives that are proving effective include programs that:

1. Expose students to entrepreneurial role models.

2. Provide hands-on experiences in creating business models and pitches.

3. Facilitate mentorship opportunities with local business leaders.

4. Encourage participation in startup incubators or competitions.

By promoting these initiatives, schools help hedge the innovative spirit of entrepreneurship into the minds of youths, preparing them not only to become future business leaders but leaders who are tuned into the needs and challenges of society.

10.3. The Community's Hand in Molding Empathetic Entrepreneurs

The impact of the community on a child's development is discussed less often than the influence of the school, but it's no less critical. We exist in a web of intricate social relationships—families, neighborhoods, cultural groups—and these are environments rich with opportunities to learn empathy.

The community's influence becomes significant when we consider social entrepreneurship, where an entrepreneurial venture's prime focus is to produce societal value. In this realm, local communities provide the knowledge and insight to empathize with societal problems deeply, thereby influencing the ideation of effective solutions.

Communities can promote empathetic entrepreneurship by:

1. Generating platforms for community service, volunteering, and social projects.

2. Encouraging local businesses to uphold community-friendly values.

3. Facilitating exchange of ideas through social events, fostering a sense of camaraderie.

4. Involving youngsters in decision-making processes at a local level, developing a sense of responsibility.

Through such initiatives, communities can significantly contribute to raising children who understand societal complexities, who care for their neighbors, and who are willing to drive change – the essence of empathetic entrepreneurship.

In conclusion, the role schools and communities take in cultivating empathetic entrepreneurs is significant in raising the next generation of leaders who perceive business as more than just a transactional endeavor. It's about nurturing individuals who understand how profound empathy can drive innovative solutions to societal problems, who appreciate that success isn't just personal but shared amongst us all.

Through a thoughtful blend of empathy and entrepreneurship education, and by providing continuous and meaningful community engagement opportunities, we can indeed nurture a generation of empathetic entrepreneurs who will not only contribute to the economic growth but also change the world for the better, one empathetic solution at a time.

Chapter 11. The Future: How Empathetic Entrepreneurs will Change the World

Our exploration of empathetic entrepreneurship leads us to ponder its impact on the future. Let us delve into the potentialities that lie within children who infuse their business aspirations with a healthy dose of empathy.

11.1. The Butterfly Effect: Small Actions, Big Impacts

The impact of empathetic entrepreneurs begins with a butterfly effect. Each child who becomes an empathetic entrepreneur contributes to a positive ripple of change. Their actions, no matter how trivial they may seem, can influence others, eventually creating tectonic shifts in societal norms and economic systems.

An example is 11-year-old Eden, whose organic lemonade stand raised not only neighborhood spirits but also a considerable sum for local homelessness charities. Although her business model was simple, Eden's mission was profound: to provide a lifeline for those who the harsh world had forgotten. Eden's operation might not have affected Wall Street, but she brought about meaningful change in her corner of the world. She's reshaping an often impersonal economic landscape into one that is personal, compassionate, and inclusive.

11.2. Empathy Meets Innovation: Creating Sustainable Solutions

Moving beyond their immediate environment, these young

empathetic entrepreneurs address global issues, innovating sustainability solutions that intersect profit and compassion.

Consider the brothers Jake and Max, 15 and 13. They transformed their concern for the world's plastic problem into a thriving ecologically-minded business. Their company, Green Toys, employs recycled plastic to manufacture a range of environmentally friendly toys. The brothers' efforts significantly reduced plastic waste and informed countless families about the urgency of environmental stewardship.

Green Toys is just one example of how empathetic entrepreneurs can repurpose commercial activity into a force for planetary resiliency. When empathy meets innovation, sustainability isn't an add-on or an afterthought—it becomes the business's foundation and its competitive advantage.

11.3. Bridging the Gap: Empathy Fuels Economic Inclusion

Economic inclusion is another societal challenge that empathetic entrepreneurs are well-positioned to address. Underserved communities often bear the brunt of economic downturns and systemic inequalities, an injustice that empathetic entrepreneurs are keen to rectify.

Take the inspiring story of 16-year-old Kavya, who created a platform connecting artisans from her native India with international markets. Understanding that these skilled crafters couldn't access lucrative markets due to limitations such as language barriers and digital literacy, she created a global online marketplace for their products.

Kavya's platform bridges economic disparities, offering artisans a fair wage and global consumers access to authentic Indian crafts. Her venture showcases the powerful change effected when empathy ignites entrepreneurial spirit.

11.4. Leading with Empathy: Revolutionizing Corporate Culture

As empathetic entrepreneurs grow and eventually transition into leaders of larger organizations, they carry their empathy-infused values. This will revolutionize corporate cultures, birthing companies that truly care for their employees, customers, and communities.

Nicole, once a teenaged empathetic entrepreneur running a neighborhood pet care service, is now the head of a leading pet care company. She integrates an "empathy first" approach, treating staff fairly with benefits like substantial healthcare and fair wages, and giving back to the community through free workshops and animal therapy sessions for local schools.

These leaders call for companies to be not only profit-oriented but also people-oriented. This shift in corporate culture is a hopeful trajectory for the world of business, a realm often criticized for ruthless, impersonal approaches.

11.5. Trailblaze into Tomorrow

Empathetic entrepreneurs envisage a world where business and compassion sit comfortably side by side, where profits don't rob but enrich communities and the environment. Their journey reminds us of the power that lies in each small action, each small business underpinned by empathy, setting in motion a cascade of change.

While it is easy to dismiss these as isolated feel-good stories, the potential societal and economic transformation they represent should not be underestimated. These young torchbearers predispose us to a future where empathy becomes the cornerstone of entrepreneurial practice, fundamentally altering trades, markets, and industries at large.

Taken together, these narratives sketch an optimistic yet realistic forecast of the arenas—economic, social, environmental—that empathetic entrepreneurs can and will influence. It encourages us, ultimately, to understand that molding our children to become empathetic entrepreneurs is not just a novel strategy for success, but a promising path to a better tomorrow.